M. Paterson 1996

KU-018-675

M. Paterson 1996

DESIGN AND MAKE
BLINDS

HEATHER LUKE

NEW HOLLAND

First published in the UK in 1995 by
New Holland (Publishers) Ltd
London • Cape Town • Sydney • Singapore

Reprinted 1996

24 Nutford Place
London W1H 6DQ
UK

P.O. Box 1144
Cape Town 8000
South Africa

3/2 Aquatic Drive
Frenchs Forest NSW 2086
Australia

Copyright © 1995 in text and blind design concepts Heather Luke
Copyright © 1995 in photographs New Holland (Publishers) Ltd
Copyright © 1995 in artwork New Holland (Publishers) Ltd
Copyright © 1995 New Holland (Publishers) Ltd

All rights reserved. No part of this publication may be reproduced,
stored in a retrieval system or transmitted, in any form or by
any means, electronic, mechanical or otherwise, without the prior written
permission of the copyright owners and publishers.

ISBN 1 85368 528 3 (hbk)
ISBN 1 85368 529 1 (pbk)

Managing Editor: Gillian Haslam
Editor: Coral Walker
Designer: Kit Johnson
Photographer: David Johnson
Illustrations: Lizzie Sanders

Typeset by Ace Filmsetting Ltd, Frome, Somerset
Reproduction by Hirt and Carter (Pty) Ltd
Printed in Malaysia by Times Offset (M) SDN BHD

ACKNOWLEDGEMENTS

My thanks to Sarah Westcott, Julie Troop and Jackie Pullman for their expert making
up, to Michael and Don for their on-site help, David Johnson for the brilliant
photographs and the team whose inspiration and magic have made the raw
materials into a book – Yvonne, Gillian and Coral at New Holland. Special thanks to
Andrew and Annie Stuart, Elizabeth Peck, Heather Phelps Brown and Jano Clark for
allowing me to show you some 'vignettes' of their lovely homes.

We would like to thank the following suppliers for their help:
Osborne and Little for the fabrics used on pages 21, 38, 76
Designers Guild for the photographs on pages 30 and 41
Mulberry page 61
Byron and Byron for the fittings on page 59
Wemyss Houles for the fittings on page 47
Artisan for the fittings on pages 24, 31
Merchants for the fittings on pages 55, 63
The Cartonnage Company for accessories on pages 62, 63, 65, 67, 69, 75

CONTENTS

INTRODUCTION

Blinds are often the ideal vehicle for attractively patterned fabrics which beg to be shown off to their full advantage. This bold, contemporary print, in earthy hues, makes a modern cascade blind.

Blinds were originally designed in the 18th century as a purely decorative feature to embellish their very practical shuttered windows. Their choice of fabric for this decorative feature highlights its many qualities as a window dressing. Firstly, fabric helps deaden noise, secondly it provides insulation from the cold outside; it also adds a dimension of cosiness, colour and texture which no other form of decoration can match.

As fabric for window treatments has developed, so the fabric itself has developed too. Today, there are endless designs of fabric, both woven and printed, along with numerous hand and machine-made trimmings, from the most basic to the most ornate.

Many fabrics today are works of art in themselves and deserve to be displayed and appreciated as such. And blinds – frequently made without fullness – offer the opportunity to enjoy the beauty of the fabric.

As well as being decorative, blinds are such a sensible window treatment – especially in rooms where water is in constant use – that even the most hardened devotees of curtaining will have to bow to their practicality. Above a kitchen sink, near a shower or bath, in a butler's pantry or utility room, blinds are the ideal option. Whether you select the totally plain and functional, or something more fun (a pleasure in a room given to daily chores), blinds offer the most practical choice.

When long curtains are preferred, but a radiator or other obstruction prevents full-length drawing curtains, I often design and make blinds to become the functioning unit, and add curtaining for style, atmosphere and balance. Various examples in this book illustrate the harmony and sympathetic relationship between blinds and curtains. Coupled with blinds, curtains can add the necessary height to a room but otherwise be solely decorative, they can be designed to create a particular atmosphere and shape, or they can be functional but only drawn with the blind once the heating has been turned off or on their own as darkness descends on a summer's evening.

Conservatories and outdoor rooms need blinds which can be made to fit different shapes and lengths, but can still be raised and lowered efficiently with a minimum of fuss. And in difficult situations, where there is little or no room above or to the sides for fabric to hang, where sill space needs to be clear, or where incoming light has to be maximised: blinds, such as flat, soft or rodded Roman blinds, prove ideal solutions.

So blinds can serve many purposes: they can be as simple or as complicated as your time and abilities allow; they can be plain and functional, decorative and functional, or just decorative. Take the basic making methods on the following pages, look at the ideas, then adapt and experiment with your own colours and thoughts to design and make your own individual blinds.

BASIC TECHNIQUES

STITCHES

Start and finish all stitching with a double stitch, never use a knot.

Hemming stitch

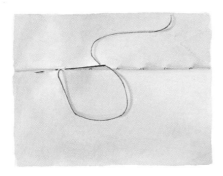

This stitch is used along hems. Each stitch should be approximately 1.5 cm (⅝ in) in length. Slide the needle through the folded hem, pick up two threads of the main fabric, and push the needle directly back into the fold.

Herringbone stitch

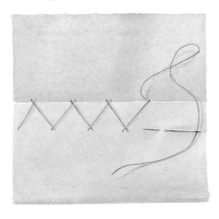

Herringbone stitch is used over any raw edge which is then covered by another fabric. It is worked in the opposite direction to all other stitches. Each stitch should be about 3 cm (1¼ in) for hems and 8 cm (3¼ in) for side turnings. Stitch into the hem, from right to left, approximately 1.5 cm (⅝ in) to the right make a stitch into the fabric picking up two threads. Pull through and stitch 1.5 cm (⅝ in) to the right making a stitch into the hem.

Ladder stitch

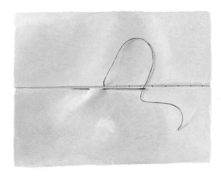

Ladder stitch is used to join two folded edges invisibly together. Slide the needle along the fold 5 mm (¼ in) and straight into the fold opposite. Slide along for 5 mm (¼ in) and back into the first fold, again directly opposite.

Long stitch

Long stitch is the most effective stitch for interlined blinds as it holds the interlining tight to the main fabric on the side turnings.

Make a horizontal stitch approximately 1 cm (⅜ in) across. Bring the thread down diagonally by about 4 cm (1½ in) and repeat.

Slip stitch

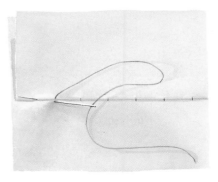

This stitch is used to sew on linings. Always use a colour thread which matches the main fabric. Make each stitch 1.5 cm (⅝ in). Slide the needle through the main fabric and pick up two threads of the lining. Push the needle back into the main fabric exactly opposite and slide through a further 1.5 cm (⅝ in).

Lock stitch

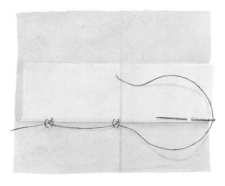

This stitch holds linings, interlinings and fabrics together, preventing them from separating, but still allowing some degree of movement. Always use thread that blends with the main fabric and the lining when stitching lining to interlining. Fold back the lining, secure the thread to the lining and make a small stitch in the main fabric just below. Make a large loop approximately 10 cm (4 in) long (slightly shorter for smaller items) and make a small stitch in the lining inside this loop. Stitch into the main fabric. Allow the stitch to remain slightly loose.

Buttonhole stitch

Work from left to right with the raw edge uppermost. Push the needle from the back to the front, 3 mm (⅛ in) below the edge. Twist the thread around the needle and pull the needle through, carefully tightening the thread so that it knots on the edge.

Blanket stitch

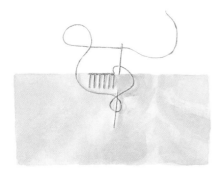

Originally used to neaten the raw edges of woollen blankets, it is now mainly decorative. It is most comfortable worked from the side with the edge towards you. Push the needle from the front to the back, about 6 mm (¼ in) from the edge (also this measurement will vary with large or small items). Hold the thread from the last stitch under the needle and pull up to make a loop on the edge.

PINNING

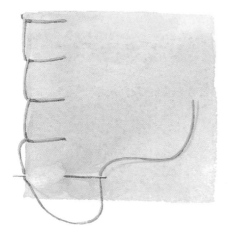

When pinning two layers of fabric together or piping on to fabric, always use horizontal and vertical pins to keep the fabric in place from both directions. The horizontal pins need to be removed just before the machine foot reaches them and the vertical ones – or cross pins – can remain in place, so the fabrics are held together the whole time.

SEAMS

Flat seam

The most common and straightforward seam for normal use. With right sides together, pin 1.5–2 cm (⅝–¾ in) in from the edge at 10 cm (4 in) intervals. Pin cross pins halfway between each seam pin. These cross pins will remain in place while you are stitching to prevent the fabrics from slipping.

Once machine-stitched, open

the seam flat and press it from the back. Turn it over and press from the front. Turn it back over once again and press from the back, under each flap, to remove the pressed ridge line.

French seam

This type of seam is very neat and leaves no raw edges. Use for sheer fabrics or any occasion when the seam might be visible.

Pin the fabrics together with the wrong sides facing. Stitch 5 mm (¼ in) from the raw edges. Trim and flip the fabric over, bringing the right sides together. Pin again, 1 cm (⅜ in) from the stitched edge and stitch along this line to enclose the raw edges. Press from the right side, always pressing the seam in one direction only.

Flat fell seam

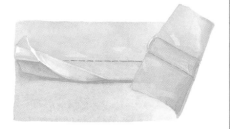

Use for neatening seams of heavier weight fabrics. Pin the fabrics together with the right sides facing and stitch 1.5–3 cm (⅝–1¼ in) from the raw edges. Trim one seam to just under half. Fold the other over to enclose the raw edge. Press down. Stitch close to the fold line.

MITRED CORNERS

This technique creates a flat and neat finish to corners.

When sides and hems are equal

1. Press the side seam over and the hem up, to the measurements given. Position a temporary pin exactly through the point of the corner.

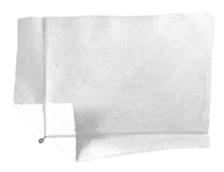

2. Open out the folds and turn in the corner at a 45° angle, with the pin at the centre of the foldline.

3. Fold the hem up and the sides in again along the original fold lines. Keep the pin on the point and make sure the fabric is firmly tucked into the folded lines.

When sides and hems are unequal

Even when this is the case, you can still achieve a neat corner. Follow step 1 as above, but when you reach step 2, the corner will not be folded to a 45° angle.

Instead, the corner will need to be angled away, towards the hem, leaving a longer fold on the side turnings so that the raw edges meet when the mitre is finished.

MAKING TIES

Ties are used throughout soft furnishings. For blinds, they are used primarily for rolled-up blinds or to tie a heading to a pole. They are also used for tying cushions and fastening loose covers.

Folded ties

Cut a strip of fabric four times the width of your finished tie and 3 cm (1¼ in) longer. Press one short end under by 1 cm (⅜ in) and both sides to the middle. Press in half, and stitch close to the fold line.

Rouleau ties

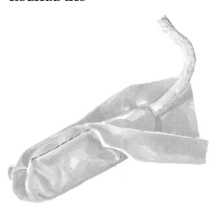

Cut a strip of fabric four times the width of your finished tie and 3 cm (1¼ in) longer. Fold in half lengthwise, right sides together, enclosing a piece of cord which is longer than the strip of fabric. Stitch along the short side to secure the cord firmly. Stitch along the length, 2 mm (⅛ in) towards the raw edge from the centre.

Trim the fabric across the corner, pull the cord through, at the same time turning the fabric right side out. Cut off the cord. Press the raw edge under and slipstitch with small stitches.

PIPING

If piping is to be used in straight lines then it will be easier to handle straight. If it is to be bent around corners, then it should be cut on the cross. For 4 mm (⅛ in) piping cord cut 4 cm (1½ in) wide strips. All joins should be made on the cross to minimise bulk.

To cut on the straight

Cut lengths as long as possible. Hold two strips, butt the ends together and trim away both corners at 45°. Hold together and flip the top one over. Stitch together where the pieces cross.

To cut on the cross

With the fabric flat on the table fold one bottom corner as if making a 30 cm (12 in) square. Cut along the fold line. Mark pencil lines from this cut edge at 4 cm (1½ in) intervals, and cut along these lines. Hold two pieces, butting the ends together as if making a continuous strip. Flip the top one over and hold. Machine stitch together where the two fabrics cross.

Making up and pinning on

Press seams flat and cut away excess corners. Fold in half along the length and insert the piping cord. Machine stitch to encase, approximately 2 mm (⅛ in) from the cord. Keep the fabric folded exactly in half.

Always pin piping so that the raw edges line up exactly with the raw edges of the main fabric.

To bend piping around curves, snip into the stitching line. To pipe around a right angle, stop pinning 1.5 cm (⅝ in) from the corner, snip the piping right to the stitching line, fold the piping to 90° and start pinning 1.5 cm (⅝ in) on the adjacent side.

Joining

To join piping, overlap by approximately 6 cm (2¼ in) and cut away excess. Unpick the casing on one side and cut away the cord so that the two ends butt up. Fold the piping fabric across at a 45° angle and cut along this fold. Fold under 1 cm (⅝ in) and pin securely before stitching.

BINDING

Binding one edge

1. Cut the binding strips to the width required. Join the strips on the cross for the required length.

2. Pin the binding to the fabric, right sides together and stitch slightly less than 1.5 cm (⅝ in) from the raw edges.

3. Neaten the raw edges to slightly less than 1.5 cm (⅝ in). Press from the front, pressing the binding away from the main fabric. Fold the binding to the back, measuring the edge to 1.5 cm (⅝ in), keeping the fabric tucked firmly into the fold and pin at approximately 8 cm (3¼ in) intervals. Turn over to the back and herringbone stitch the edge of the binding to the main fabric, or fold under again.

Binding a corner

If you need to bind a corner, mitre the binding. Stop pinning just short of the corner by the width of the finished binding. Fold the binding back on itself to make a sharp 45° angle and pin across this fold line. Continue to pin on the adjacent side, the same distance from the edge. Stitch the binding on, stopping right on the pin and secure stitching. Begin stitching again at the same point, on the adjacent side. Press to mitre, and fold the fabric to the back, mitring the corner in the opposite direction to relieve the bulk.

DESIGNING YOUR BLIND

The length of a blind is almost always determined by the depth of the window, the position of the sill or a radiator beneath. The width of a blind is determined by the basic design chosen, how much fullness is to be included in any swags, and how the blind looks in proportion to the window when it is raised.

If a blind is part of an overall design for the window treatment it will probably fit against the window, from the inside of the reveal to the sill and be relatively insignificant. If it is the whole window dressing, and therefore of greater importance to the room design, it might well be fitted in front of the reveal or frame, and may well have added detail in the form of shaped hems or sides which need to be shown to achieve the full effect.

Swagged blinds can be made with almost any degree of fullness, which will govern the drop of the swag. The easiest and most accurate way to be sure of the design is to draw the effect you would like to see to scale, transfer it to the window and then measure the swags.

This exercise in design is surprisingly simple to do, will give you much more confidence with your ideas and will in the end produce better and more interesting blinds. You just need the basic width and drop of the window to be dressed, scaled

down to fit a piece of graph paper, with pieces of tracing paper to cover on to which you can sketch some ideas. Once you have a window treatment which you like, transfer the measurements to the actual window to check. Use a length of tape or string to judge the depth and amount of swags for gathered blinds, and newspaper or brown paper to make templates of possible hem shapes.

Adding a shaped hem to the bottom of a plain roller blind can transform the rather ordinary into an attractive feature. Use one of the shapes above as a guide and apply the hem to the blind as described on page 18.

UNUSUAL WINDOWS

Not all windows are neat-and-tidy rectangles or squares, set into a vertical wall. Unusually shaped or awkwardly positioned windows always tax the designer's imagination, how to dress them without spoiling the shape, where and how to hang the fittings. And how to tackle windows set into sloping eaves. Try some of these ideas if you have a less than ordinary window shape.

Gothic windows are actually better with no fabric covering but there are times when a simple cover is required. A blind which is shaped to fit the frame but fits at the bottom of the window out of the way when not needed was our solution to this problem. We decided to use a simple fabric which would not detract from the window wood or shape. This same idea can be adapted to almost any difficult shaped window, whether hexagonal, octagonal or triangular which need little or occasional covering. The line of the frame is completely undisturbed, the cover could be left either attached to the lower rod and hooks or folded away when not in use.

Sloping windows are also difficult to dress. Blinds can easily be fitted in place with a ratchet system to control the level at which the blind is dropped. However the window area often looks bare so needs to be dressed with curtaining or draped fabrics. A first floor bedroom in a barn conversion left me with these problem windows. My brief was to create a romantic, feminine room from a vast space, so we first covered the walls in a fabric reminiscent of a cottage garden, especially printed for me in France and then canopied the bed in silk and lace. Overlong silk curtains tied back softened the window. Roller blinds covered to match the walls were made and fitted inside the window reveal, functioning perfectly, but as unobtrusively as possible, still allowing the draped fabrics to take first place.

Odd windows rarely occur in new properties and are never part of an original design. But unfortunately many old houses have been adapted to different uses throughout their history.

Long thin windows in the corner of a room are the result of a larger room and a larger window being split into two. Roman blinds are a good solution for these windows – fitted into the recess they take up little room and may be left partly down to help redress the balance in the room.

But two windows of completely different styles, shapes or levels pose more of a problem for an ideal design solution. Roman blinds, as basically flat pieces of fabric, can go some way to disguising the differences in proportion, especially if an attention-seeking design is used (see right). A good solution is to wallpaper the room with an all-over pattern and then to make blinds which pattern-match. This ensures a continuity of design when the blinds are lowered.

Left: For those that dislike blinds as a window dressing but are unable to use anything else as a functional unit, this treatment is ideal. The blind pulls up behind the feminine curtains which are extremely pretty but purely decorative. **Below left and below:** A simple flat blind has been designed to the shape of the window which can be rolled up from the bottom and held in place with tabs. **Bottom:** The unsettling proportions of these windows have been remedied by pattern matching at eye level.

FITTINGS FOR BLINDS

Most fabric blinds are fixed to wooden battens which hold the fittings necessary to operate them. The headings, whether flat, pleated or gathered, must be made up to fit the batten size. Touch and close tape is usually used to hold the blind to the batten, with one piece stapled or tacked to the batten and the other stitched to the back of the blind heading. Small coloured tacks may also be used to fit the blind to the batten.

Roller blinds have a roller and fixing brackets included in the kit. Make sure that you follow the manufacturer's instructions when assembling the blind.

Rolled up blinds will fit to a batten as discussed above, but instead rely on attached tapes, cords or ribbons to raise and lower them to the position required.

Cascade, Roman, London, Austrian and festoon blinds all depend on a series of cords threaded through rings at regular intervals across the blind to operate them.

Each blind design will require different spacings between the cords, and this will be planned with the overall design. The instructions for making up generally show where and how the rings on the blinds should be fitted and how the cords need to be fixed and threaded through the rows of rings.

MAKING THE BATTEN

Cut a piece of wood 5 × 2 cm (2 × ¾ in) to the finished width of the blind design. Cut a length of fabric 4 cm (1½ in) longer than this and 15 cm (6 in) wider. Apply glue to the back of the batten (one of the 5 cm/2 in sides) and wrap the fabric tightly around. Staple or tack one side of some touch and close tape to the top at the front of the batten. Stitch the other piece of touch and close tape to the blind heading. The batten is now ready to be fitted to the blind.

Mark the batten in line with the rows of rings and the cords. Take the blind away and fit either brass screw eyes or china thimbles at these points, to carry the cords.

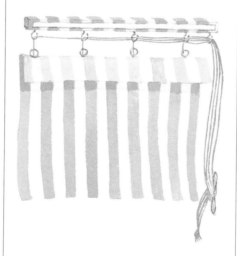

You will now need to decide from which side you prefer to operate the blind. Fit the batten in position on the window and fit the cleat which will hold the cords in a convenient opposition. Thread the cords through, starting with the side away from the operating fittings. Thread the first cord through all the rings to the opposite side of the blind, the second cord through the next ring, and so on.

When you have threaded through all the cords, hold them together and pull the blind up as high as possible. Adjust the pleats, raise and lower the blind at least two or three times to ensure that the cords are free and the blind hangs straight.

With the blind lowered, knot the cords together at the bottom of the cleat. Raise the blind, secure the cords and adjust the pleats, folds or gathers. Check now that the blind is still hanging straight and if it is not, re-tie the cords. Thread the cords into a cord weight, knot and trim away the excess.

Blinds can also be fitted to poles, but the same batten will need to be fitted just behind the pole so that the blind can be raised and lowered efficiently.

The size of the batten should be altered to suit your situation. Blinds may be fitted flat against the frame, or forwards to avoid window fittings. Fit into the ceiling, the window frame or with small brackets.

Possible positions of batten

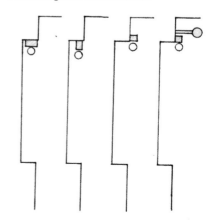

MEASURING FOR BLINDS

Once you have chosen the design of the blind and the position of the fittings, take accurate measurements to find the finished width and the overall drop. Final measurements can only be taken once the fittings are in place, but an estimate will enable you to order the fabric required.

If the building is newly built and access to the window is not possible, use the builder's drawings to estimate fabrics, but leave the making up until all building works are complete.

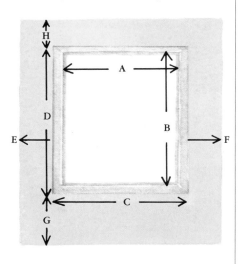

A = width of window frame, B = height of window frame, C = width of window reveal, D = height of window reveal, E = space to the left, F = space to the right, G = space below the sill, H = space above the reveal

As all blinds need to be raised and lowered without interruption, they need to be made exactly 'square'. Very few windows have four corners which are absolute right angles, so use a set square or spirit level to determine the top

line. Lightly pencil the top line on the frame or wall from which the measurements will be taken and to which the batten will be fitted. Measure at 20 cm (8 in) intervals both the width and the drop. The narrowest or shortest measurement is the one which you must use to be sure that the blind can be raised and lowered without trouble.

Special care needs to be taken with cottage or very old windows, where the opening or blind space may vary considerably with uneven walls and plastering.

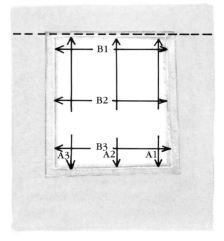

A1 = 102 cm (40 in), B1 = 64 cm (25 in),
A2 = 102.5 cm (40¼ in), B2 = 65 cm (25½ in),
A3 = 103 cm (40½ in), B3 = 64 cm (25 in).
So the blind should be made 102 × 64 cm
(40 × 25 in)

Most blinds can be made to fit windows with shaped tops, for example, arches, although round windows are more difficult.

The easiest arched tops to work with have a fairly shallow curve. The blind will only pull up to the bottom of the curve, so consider the amount of available light which might be taken away.

You will need to mark a

horizontal line as near to the bottom of the arched shape as possible. Cut a paper template of

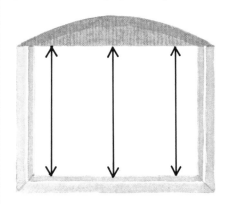

this arch, using the line you've just drawn as the bottom of the template. Measure from this line to the sill, or bottom of the blind.

If you want to make cascade, Austrian or festoon blinds, you will need to know how full they will be. Again use a strip of fabric, piece of string or length of lightweight chain and tape this to the window to see the sort of hem shape you can make (below). When you are happy with the shape, remove the tape and measure the total length and the length of each swag. This will be the finished width, which is the width the blind needs to be made.

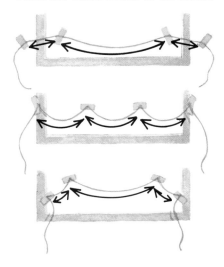

ESTIMATING FABRIC

Regardless of the size of your window, each style of blind will require a different quantity of fabric depending on the style of blind you choose. A rolled-up blind, for example, will need much less fabric than a festoon blind – which can use up to 200 per cent more width and 300 per cent more depth than the window measurement. The cost of the fabric may determine your choice of blind, although the style of room and furnishings will be your first guide.

Use the following examples to help you estimate the amount of fabric you will require for each blind treatment.

ROMAN BLINDS

Decide whether the blind is to fit inside the window reveal, against the frame or outside the reveal, to the wall or an outer frame. To the finished width and the overall drop add 12 cm (4¾ in) for the side turnings and 6 cm (2¼ in) for the hem, plus heading allowance of 2–3 cm (¾–1¼ in).

1. To determine amount of fabric:
Example – finished width 150 cm (60 in) and overall drop 200 cm (79 in):

Each cut length will be:
200 cm + 3 cm + 6 cm = 209 cm
(79 in + 1¼ in + 2 ¼ in = 82½ in)
The number of widths needed will depend on the width of your fabric, say 130 cm (51 in).
So, 150 cm + 12 cm = 162 cm ÷ 130 cm = 1.24 (60 in + 4¾ in = 64¾ ÷ 51 in = 1.25), say 2.
2 × 209 cm = 418 cm (2 × 82½ in = 165 in or 4½ yd).

2. You will now need to determine the size of the folds:
This will affect the amount of space taken up by the blind when it is pulled up. As a general rule of thumb, aim to make a blind which will take up approximately 17–19 cm (7–7½ in) of space when folded up.

Bear in mind that you will be stitching a rod at the top of each fold. The distance between the rods will be 30–34 cm (12–13½ in). The lowest section should be 1–2 cm (⅜–¾ in) more than half the distance between each rod.

Take the finished drop of the blind and deduct 2 cm (¾ in). Divide the rest by approximately 15 cm (6 in). You will need an uneven number, so try dividing by amounts between 15–17 cm (6–7 in) until you have a satisfactory figure.
Example: Finished length of blind will be 116 cm (45½ in)
116 cm − 2cm = 114 cm (45½ in − ¾ in = 44¾ in)
114 cm ÷ 15 cm = 7.60 cm (44¾ in ÷] 6 in = 7½ in)
Using 7 as the nearest uneven number, 114 cm ÷ 7 cm = 16.29 cm (44¾ in ÷ 7 in = 6½ in.
The folds of the blind will be 16.29 cm + 2 cm (6½ in + ¾ in) for the lower section and 32.58 cm (12½ in) for each of the other sections. Round these figures up to 18.3 cm and 32.6 cm (7 in and 13 in).

This example requires three folds and therefore three rods. (The lining cuts will need to include 6 cm (2¼ in) extra for each rod pocket.)

CASCADE BLINDS

To the finished width and overall drop measurements you will need to add 20–24 cm (8–9½ in) for the side turnings and 12–17 cm (4¾–6¾ in) for the hem, plus heading allowances. Add a further 3 cm per 50 cm (1¼ in per 20 in) on average, or 5 cm (2 in) for each scallop to give a little fullness.

1. To calculate fullness needed:
Example: the blind finished width is 140 cm (55 in) with three scallops of 34 cm (14 in) and two sides of 19 cm (7½ in).
Add the side turning allowances to the width:
140 cm + 22 cm + 22 cm = 184 cm (55 in + 9 in + 9 in = 73 in)
Add fullness (5 cm/2 in either side of each scallop):
4 × 5 = 20 cm + 184 cm = 204 cm
Divide this figure by the width of the fabric, say 135 cm (53 in).
204 cm ÷ 135 cm = 1.5 (80 in ÷ 53 in = 1.5)
so allow two widths of fabric for each blind.
The overall drop required is 185 cm (73 in)
Add the hem and heading allowances
185 cm + 12 cm + 6 cm = 203 cm (73 in + 4¾ in + 2¼ in = 80 in)
So you will need two lengths of 203 cm (80 in) 2 × 203 cm = 406 cm (2 × 80 in = 160 in.
Allow 4.5 m (4½ yd) of fabric

FESTOON BLINDS

Festoon blinds have most of their fullness in the length, some have a little fullness in the width and some are also gathered widthwise. You must choose the number of swags, the finished width of the blind and the fullness for each swag. Add 6 cm (2¼ in) for each side turning. Add the heading allowance and 2 cm (¾ in) to the length.

Example: finished width 128 cm (50 in) and overall drop of 170 cm (67 in). The festoon blind will have four swags with one and a half times fullness across the width and double the fullness in the length.

Each cut length will be:
170 cm × 2 cm = 340 cm + 6 cm headings + 2 cm hem = 348 cm
(67 in × 2 = 134 in + 2¼ in + ¾ in = 137 in)

For the swags:
32 cm × 1.5 = 48 cm × 4 = 192 cm + sides 12 cm + turnings 12 cm = 226 cm (12½ in × 1.5 = 18¾ in × 4 = 75 in + 4¾ in + 4¾ in = 84½ in)
Divide by the width of your fabric, say 130 cm (51 in):
226 ÷ 130 = 1.73 (84½ in ÷ 51 in = 1.65 in)
So you will need two lengths of 348 cm (137 in) = 696 cm (274 in)
Allow 7 m (7½ yd) of fabric.

LONDON BLINDS

From your plan you will know how many swags to allow. Pleats should require approximately the same again.
Example: overall drop 200 cm (79 in), finished width 130 cm (51 in) with three swags of 32 cm (12½ in) and two sides of 18 cm (7 in).
Each cut length will be:
200 cm + hems 10 cm + headings 2–3 cm = 213 cm
(79 in + 4 in + ¾ – 1¼ in = 84 in)
Swags: 3 × 32 cm = 96 cm + sides 36 cm + turnings 36 cm + pleats [4 × 30 cm = 120 cm] = 288 cm
(3 × 12½ in = 37½ in + 14 in + 14 in + pleats [4 × 12 in = 48 in] = 113½ in
Divide by the fabric width, say 130 cm (51 in):
288 cm ÷ 130 cm = 2.21 (113½ in ÷ 51 in = 2.22)
So you will need three lengths of 213 cm (84 in) = 639 cm (252 in)
Allow 6.5 m (7 yd) of fabric.

PATTERN REPEATS

Each cut length must include complete pattern repeats.
Example: Length needed 200 cm (79 in), pattern repeat 45 cm (18 in). Divide the length by the pattern repeat: 200 cm ÷ 45 cm = 4.44 (79 in ÷ 18 in = 4.38)
so 5 pattern repeats will be needed for each cut, making each length 45 cm × 5 = 225 cm (18 in × 5 = 90 in)

AUSTRIAN BLINDS

Austrian blinds are really pull-up curtains, with fullness added to the width and gathers or pleats incorporated at the heading to fit the batten width. Approximately 30 cm (12 in) added to the overall drop allows the bottom edge to remain swagged when the blind is lowered. Add approximately 12 cm (4¾ in) for the side turnings.
Example: finished width 130 cm (50 in), overall drop 200 cm (79 in):
Each cut length will be:
200 cm + 30 cm + hem 12 cm + heading 6 cm = 248 cm (79 in + 12 in + 4¾ in + 2¼ in = 98 in).
From the plan you will know how many swags and how much fullness each will have.

For this example, the blind has five swags of 30 cm (12 in), two sides of 10 cm (4 in), and the draped cord shows that each swag should have a 50 cm curve (20 in).
Swags: 50 cm × 5 = 250 cm + sides 10 cm × 2 = 20 cm + turnings of 20 cm = 290 cm (20 in × 5 = 100 in + 4 in × 2 = 8 in + 8 in = 116 in).
Divide this measurement by the width of your fabric (say, 130 cm (51 in) to determine the number of widths
290 cm ÷ 130 cm = 2.23 (116 in ÷ 51 in = 2.27
So you will need three lengths of 248 cm (98 in) = 744 cm (294 in)
Allow 7.5 m (8½ yd) of fabric.

PREPARATION

Preparation is the key to successful sewing. Prepare well, and the work should go smoothly, with few errors.

Look at various factors before you begin: where you are going to work, what you plan to work on, where you intend hanging the fabric while you work, the fabric you plan to use, linings and interlinings. Check over your equipment. Make sure your sewing machine is running smoothly. Scrutinize needles and pins, discarding any that are rusty or blunt. Make sure that you have the correct thread and sufficient for your needs. Poor tools will give poor results. Here are some guidelines to bear in mind before you begin sewing.

THE WORKTABLE

If possible, you should stake your claim on one room which can be put aside for your use only, even if it is only while you are making your blinds.

A dining room or guest bedroom can be made into a temporary workroom with little effort. A worktable which is at least 2.5 × 1.2 m (8 × 4 ft) and preferably 3 × 1.5 m (10 × 5 ft) will make the whole job so much easier. You can buy a sheet of board in either of these sizes. If you cover your dining table with thick felt, the board can be rested on top.

Alternatively, make some sturdy legs which can be bracketed on to the underside of the board. This quickly-made table can then be fitted temporarily over a guest bed. The space below can be used to store all your fabrics and the top will be wide enough for you to work on a whole width of fabric at a time. Pure luxury compared to hands and knees on the floor!

The height of the worktable should be whatever is comfortable for you; I use a table that is 95 cm (38 in) high.

Cover the top with heavy interlining and then a layer of lining. Staple these to the underside; pulling the fabrics taut as you go. You will now have a soft surface which is ideal for pinning and pressing.

CUTTING OUT

Before you begin to cut the fabric, check it thoroughly for flaws. In a large amount of fabric there are likely to be some flaws, so try to cut around simple line flaws or incorporate them into headings and hems. If the fabric is badly flawed, return it to the retailer.

Measure out each length and mark with pins to make sure that you have the correct amount of fabric and always double check your measurements before making any cuts.

Fabric should ideally be cut along the grain and to pattern, but sometimes the printing method allows the pattern to move off grain. Do not be tempted to follow the pattern and cut off

grain, as the blinds will then not hang straight. As you cut each piece, mark the right sides and the direction of a plain piece of fabric just in case there is a weave variation which is not noticeable until the blinds have been made up and hung.

Try not to fold your lengths at all, but if you do need to fold them, make sure it is always lengthwise. We have a series of poles fitted to the wall of the workroom over which each length is hung until it is ready for use. You might have a bannister rail, for example, which could serve the same purpose.

Join the widths and half widths as planned, using flat seams for all lined and interlined blinds and a flat fell seam for unlined blinds.

Always keep a full width in the centre and make joins to either side. Trim away any writing on the selvedge, press from the back and then from the front. Press again on the back, with the toe of the iron between the seam and the front fabric to remove any pressing lines.

FABRIC WITH BORDERS

Some fabrics have printed or woven borders on one or both sides, so before cutting you need to determine where and how to use them. Usually borders look better on blinds around the edges rather than on the seams, so cut away all borders before joining the widths and then stitch back on to the blind – at the hem only, on both sides and hem, or all around.

PATTERN MATCHING

1. Place one of the cuts of fabric right side facing up on to the worktable with the selvedge facing you. Place the next cut over the first, right side down. Fold over the selvedge showing approximately 5 mm (¼ in) of the pattern and press lightly.

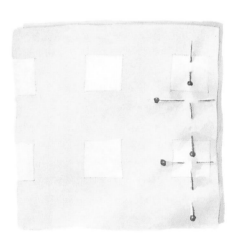

2. Match the pattern to the piece underneath, and pin through the fold line along the whole length. You may need to ease one of the sides at times – using more pins will help. Go back and place cross pins between each pin. Machine or hand stitch along the fold line, removing the straight pins and stitching over the cross pins.

3. Press the seam from the wrong side and then again from the front. Use a very hot iron and press quickly. Turn over again to the back and press under the seam to remove the pressed ridges. If the background fabric is dark or you are using a woven fabric, snip into the selvedges at approximately 5 cm (2 in) intervals. If the background fabric is light, trim the selvedges back to 1.5 cm (⅝ in), removing any writing.

LININGS

Buy good quality lining as it will wear well; an important point with blinds which, in many cases, are raised and lowered at least twice a day.

Cut out your lining fabric as close to the grain as possible. Because this is often hard to see, allow approximately 5 cm (2 in) extra for each piece. Join all lining widths with flat seams.

Buy lining the same width as your main fabric or if the lining is wider, cut down to match the fabric width before joining.

Soft (unrodded) blinds

Wherever possible, the lining seams must match the fabric seams. Apart from helping to keep the fabrics straight, all seams show up against the light when the blinds are in position, so the making methods must be as neat and unobtrusive as possible.

Press all seams flat both front and back to remove any ridges, fold linings lengthwise and rest over a long table or bannister rail to keep everything straight.

Rodded blinds

Cut the lining lengths to the length of the finished blind plus 6 cm (2¼ in) for each rod pocket. Join widths to match the main fabric, and trim to exactly the finished blind width. Place the lining on to the worktable with the right side facing down. Press over 3 cm (1¼ in) along each long side.

Starting from the bottom, and using the set square, trim the hemline exactly square with the two sides. Measure from this line up to mark the position of the lower rod pocket, in two rows 5 cm (2 in) apart. Use a set square to keep these lines exactly at right angles to the sides.

Measure from this line to the next, then 6 cm (2¼ in) and repeat to the top. Check that the distance between the top of the blind and the top of the top rod pocket is correct.

Draw a light pencil line at the top and bottom of each rod pocket. Fold together and stitch one each in turn. Press the rod pockets upwards and leave on one side.

INTERLININGS

Cut the interlining the same size as the linings as it will be trimmed to the exact size of the finished blind during the making. Use only the sarille interlining or a light to medium weight cotton bump. Interlining gives a good, soft, finish but should not be too obviously thick and padded. Join all widths with flat seams and trim back to 1.5 cm (⅝ in).

ROLLER BLINDS

Roller blinds can be made at home using your own fabric to match or tone with your other soft furnishings. You will need first to purchase a roller blind kit, available from specialist curtain fittings suppliers or large department stores. This kit will contain the rod and window fixings, the bottom batten, cord and a cord holder. You will need to make your fabric rigid enough to hang straight in the window yet flexible enough to be able to roll up neatly. A special stiffening spray or paste will be available from the same suppliers. Sometimes you can buy specially stiffened fabrics or Holland linen which are ideal if you just want to use the blind to protect furnishings from the sunlight; but if the blind is to be a feature in its own right, then you will probably want to use your own choice of colour and design.

The main advantage with a roller blind is that the roller can easily be fitted behind a pelmet, another blind, or a fixed curtain heading, to pull up completely out of sight. (A good example, for those wanting a purely functional blind which can be totally hidden, appears on page 13.) Also, if you only have a very small window in the house and wish to retain as much light as possible, roller blinds will fit right into the recess, against the window and will pull up into the depth of the top window frame.

Usually the roller blind is fitted so that the roller is in front of the blind when it is down. You can, however, change this. If the spring mechanism is reverse rolled, the roll will be behind the blind and therefore invisible.

I often make a small covered 'pelmet' board in the same fabric and fit it in front of the top of the blind so that the 'mechanics' are completely hidden. Just cover a 10 cm (4 in) deep piece of wood or MDF board with the chosen fabric, fix small brackets to the back, and screw into the ceiling in front of the blind.

MAKING UP

1. You must cut the fabric so that it fits between the fittings. This will be narrower than the measured width, so cut the roller to size first. Finish the edge with a straight or zigzag stitch to prevent the edges fraying.

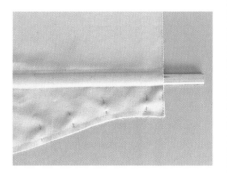

2. Shape the lower edge as you wish. Make a facing and attach it to the back of the hem. Stitch a pocket for the rod and stitch together at the lower edge to strengthen. Test the batten for fit.

3. Take the fabric outside and spray or paste with the stiffening solution. Leave to dry.

4. On the worktable, press the fabric. Check with your set square and with the sides and end of the table, that the top of the blind is absolutely square. Remove the sticky tape from the roller bar and carefully position the top of the blind along the marked line. Be careful not to stretch the fabric at all. Fix in position with small upholstery gimp pins.

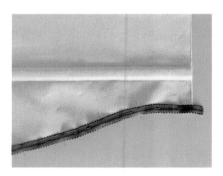

5. Add any trimming to the lower edge and glue in place. Hold with cross pins until the glue dries.

An attractive patterned roller blind with a gently scalloped edge serves to keep out the morning light, allowing the soft muslin to filter the sunlight during the day.

ROLLED UP BLINDS

This wonderful decoy duck print is displayed at its best used flat, in this rolled up blind. Lengths of green garden cord were plaited together and threaded between brass eyelets to raise and lower the blind.

Ideal for children's bedrooms, bathrooms, cloakrooms, conservatories, guest bedrooms, halls and any small windows which are awkward to dress, rolled up blinds can be fitted inside or outside the window recess and be made as full or as flat as you wish. For the novice, these blinds are a very good place to start. They may be lined or unlined, and can easily be completely hand-sewn – so even if you don't possess a sewing machine, you can still make a good window treatment.

Rolled up blinds operate with tapes which tie at the bottom of the blind at whichever level you choose to leave it. The only drawback to using these blinds is that if your window is high, you will need to be able to stand on a chair to pull it right up, and while this might be acceptable for occasional use, it will prove very inconvenient for everyday use. Cascade blinds are very similar to make, but they have rings and cords to operate them. However, just extend these instructions to make a cascade blind.

Experiment with different edgings, borders, linings in contrast colourings, different patterns and pull the blind up with fabric ties, ribbons, tapes, string, soft belts or anything else which seems suitable. Think also about the top fittings: instead of flat fastening tape, use brass eyelets with string, metal hooks, wooden pegs or ribbon ties.

MAKING UP

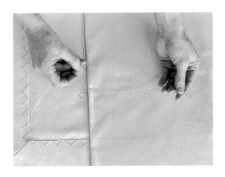

1. Add 25 cm (10 in) to the width of the fitting and cut the fabric and lining following the instructions on page 17. Place the fabric on to the worktable, wrong side facing up. Press the sides over by 12 cm (4¾ in) and the hem by the same amount. Mitre the corners following the instructions on page 8. Herringbone the raw edges along both sides and hem, ladder stitching the mitre.

The duck print blind (page 21) is neatly raised and lowered with these threaded cords: a simple, but very effective, device.

2. Place the lining over the top fabric, matching the seams. Lock stitch the lining to the main fabric on each seam and three times across each width.

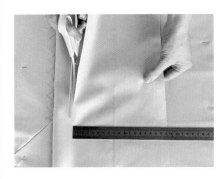

3. Using the scissors, score the lining along the folded edges of the blind. Trim the excess lining 8 cm (3¼ in) away from this line.

4. Fold the edges of the lining under by 2 cm (¾ in) to leave 10 cm (4 in) of main fabric showing on the sides and hem. Neatly slip stitch in place.

5. Carefully measure up from the hem at 30 cm (12 in) intervals to mark the overall drop. Pin in a line along the overall drop and then make the heading.

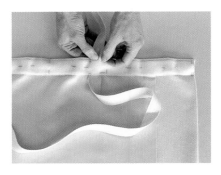

6. The usual fitting for flat blinds is touch and close tape. Trim the fabric to 1.5 cm (⅝ in) above the overall drop line, fold over and press. Pin on the touch and close tape and machine in place. Stitch ties, tapes or ribbons in place.

WARDROBE DOORS

I recently had these storage shelves built against a spare wall along a corridor, to hold out-of-season clothes, shoes, occasional hats and party wear. Fabric-covered boxes were made to be attractive on the shelves, but I wanted the option to cover the whole front. Conventional doors were not suitable due to restrictions of economy and space, so I designed these rolled-up blinds to be made from inexpensive artists' linen and bound them with curtain heading tape for an effective, economical solution.

DESIGN AND MAKE BLINDS

HOOKS AND TIES

1. A row of wrought iron pigs make amusing hooks to hold this kitchen blind in place. Checked fabrics always look just that bit smarter finished with a binding, whether plain or in self-fabric cut on the cross.

For a 3 cm (1¼ in) border, cut strips on the cross 12 cm (4¾ in) wide. Stitch together to make one length which will fit all around the blind and follow the instructions for binding edges on page 9. Stitch 3 cm (1¼ in) from the raw edges and take care to keep the checks lined up, whether on the straight or on the cross.

Make ties from cross-cut fabric, following the instructions on page

8. Take care not to stretch the bias edge; always press straight down rather than pushing the iron along the fabric, and use the largest machine stitch.

This blind can be made easily into a curtain by using the same ties to catch the fabric back to one side. This method of fitting is ideal if a window covering is needed only occasionally, perhaps in a guest bedroom.

2. Thirty per cent extra fabric was added to the blind fitting width to produce the swagged hemline. The extra fullness has been contained at the heading in four inverted pleats. Lining the chintz with a striped fabric, picking up the same red and green tones, gives an interesting finish when the blind is rolled up.

3. Checks and stripes have been used together ever since fabric was first woven and they still always look good combined within one room or one window treatment. The size, colour and balance of scale allow stripes and checks to look either very sophisticated or traditionally country in style.

The attached pelmet heading was lined and made up in the same way as the blind and stitched along the top with the front of the heading against the lining of the blind, folded to the front and pressed. Eyelet holes were cut at equal intervals across the top of the blind and eyelets fitted following the manufacturer's instructions supplied with the kit.

CASCADE BLINDS

Cotton duck was laundered first to soften the rather crisp fabric. Blue and white striped piping was then stitched to the sides and hem, adding enough weight to give some shape and just a touch of detail.

Cascade blinds differ from rolled up blinds by the way they are raised and lowered. These blinds have rings stitched to the back in rows. Strings or cords are threaded through the rings and these operate the blind. The number of rows governs the number of swags and the width of each one, while the vertical distance between the rings determines the size of the pleats and folds.

Cascade blinds are informal in character. A little fullness to the fitting width is allowed for each swag (allow 3 cm [1¼ in] for a shallow swag and up to 8 cm [3¼ in] for a deeper one.) Just one rod is stitched along the lower edge to hold the blind straight. Often this rod is made narrower than the blind width to encourage the sides to fold casually and to droop a little. Refer to pages 13–15 for instructions on estimating and measuring.

MAKING UP

1. Place fabric on to the work-table, right side facing down. Fold over the sides by 10–20 cm (4–8 in) depending on how much drop you want to see at each side; fold up the hem by 12 cm (4¾ in). Mitre the corners following instructions on page 8. Cut away the excess fabric inside the corners by first trimming off the triangle of fabric, as shown.

2. Cut away the remaining excess fabric, as shown, to give a neat finish. Hold the corners up to the light to make sure that there are only parallel lines of fabric showing through.

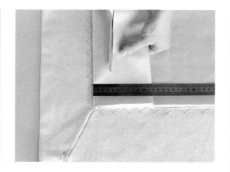

3. Herringbone stitch all the raw edges and ladder stitch along the mitred corner. Place lining over, matching seams. Fold back along the herringboned edges and trim 4 cm (2½ in) from the fold.

4. Fold lining under by 2 cm (¾ in) and pin down.

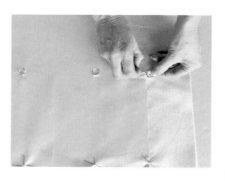

5. Mark the ring positions with crossed pins, measuring carefully between each one. Stitch each ring securely in place.

6. Measure at 30 cm (12 in) intervals from the hemline to the top to mark the overall drop line. Fold over along this line and trim the excess fabric to 1.5 cm (⅝ in) from the folded line. Pin touch and close tape in position and stitch in place along both sides.

7. Thread the cords from the bottom to the top of the blind, making sure they are long enough to return to the cord holder. Stitch the ends of the cords together to prevent the knots coming undone. Cut a wooden or metal rod, cover with lining and stitch in line with the bottom ring position along the top of the hemline. This will hold the blind straight at the bottom.

Even though the window is small, the large scale pattern works well because the recess is deep. The choice of vase sitting on the sill also echoes the traditional print. Cascade blinds are ideal to use in a recess. Fully raised, they block very little light and do not clutter the sill in operation.

One of the most exciting aspects of designing and making soft furnishings is the mixing of fabrics, textures and patterns. A rich tomato and ochre checked blind provides an unusual foil for the traditional floral curtains. These heavy curtains can remain tied back in the summer months with the blinds being lowered for privacy.

If no fullness is added to the blind width, the blind falls absolutely flat and will pull inwards as it is raised. A richly patterned fabric draws attention to the design and colourings, looking dramatic where a plain fabric might look rather boring. In this case (right) cords and rings are stitched behind the stripes to be invisible and give the blind three scallops when pulled up. Narrow binding in blue picks up the deepest tone in the print.

Bold patterned fabric benefits from the gentle folds of the cascade blind, which barely distorts the image.

FORMAL CASCADES

More formal cascade blinds (below) can be made if there is no fullness added to the width and the rows of rings and cords to pull up the blind are stitched closely enough together to prevent the fabric dipping in between. The edges are piped to stiffen them and the bottom edge is held straight with a covered wooden or metal rod.

A shortened rod allows the sides to pleat in smaller gathers as the blind is raised and lowered. This adds interest with detracting from the uncluttered lines. Five rows of rings and cords set at 20 cm (8 in) intervals operate the blind and control the form.

MAKING A PIPED EDGE

1. Cut away the amount allowed for the sides, facing or turnings. Make up enough piping, pin and stitch to the front of the blind. Stitch the borders and hem back to the blind, leaving the corners open.

2. Press the facings back, pin and cut across the corners to mitre.

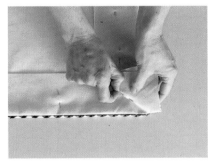

3. Slipstitch across the mitre and herringbone the raw edges.

ROMAN BLINDS

The Roman blind in this window treatment does the work while the two layers of outer curtains provide the dressing, picking up the colours of the blind in opposing intensities.

Roman blinds are a neat and smart answer to difficult windows where there is no room for the curtains to stack back. They are also useful where windows need to be covered on a budget, as Roman blinds need less than half the fabric required for curtains. If light is a problem they can easily be fixed above the window, thereby letting in the maximum amount of light when pulled up. Roman blinds are often used in conjunction with dress curtains where a radiator is fitted directly beneath the window. In this situation, only the blinds can be pulled down at night. Roman blinds are often interlined to give extra insulation and a slightly 'padded' look which is attractive.

A Roman blind should never be more than 220 cm (86 in) wide. The rods will start to bend and the blind will not pull up evenly beyond this width. It is especially important to choose good quality, firm fabric for a wide blind, and one which will not pucker when sewn. Avoid large patterns and any design which will look unbalanced when the blind is folded up. Stripes can be awkward to make up. Check that the stripe widths work with the blind width, as stripes should be shown complete, wherever possible. Checks look smart and give good stitching guidance. It is essential that any geometric pattern is printed or woven on the straight of the grain.

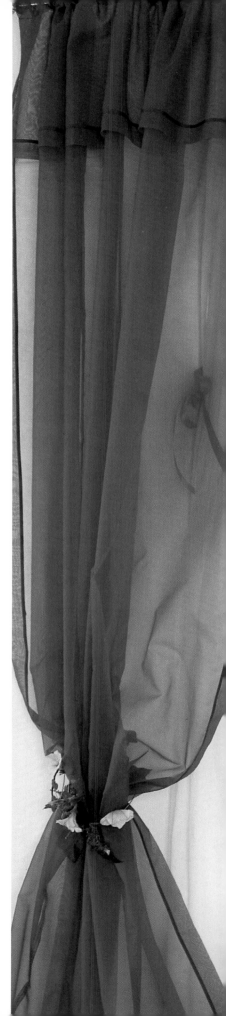

MAKING UP

1. Press the sides of the lining 3 cm (1¼ in) to the wrong side and pin in place. Cut the hemline of the lining straight, using either the set square or two sides of the worktable for accuracy.

2. Using a soft pencil or vanishing marker, measure up from the hemline and mark the stitching lines for the rod pockets. Pin the folds and stitch in place, keeping the sides even and stitching from one direction to prevent the fabric pulling.

3. Place the main fabric right side facing down on to the worktable, flatten it out with a metre rule or yardstick and turn in the sides by 6 cm (2¼ in). Turn up the 6 cm (2¼ in) hem allowance and fold the bottom corner over to mitre.

4. Leave open, but herringbone the sides and hem.

5. If the blind is to be interlined, place the interlining on top of the main fabric before turning in the sides. Fold the sides over and press. Unfold and trim the interlining back to the folded lines. Herringbone the interlining to the fold lines. Continue to follow the instructions, making up the main fabric and interlining as one.

6. Place the lining over the main fabric, pockets outwards. Carefully line up seams and hemline. Pin the sides securely. Pin each of the pocket stitching lines to the blind with pins at right angles to the stitching and with the pockets facing upwards. Slip stitch the sides between the pockets.

7. Machine stitch along the pocket lines, stitching from one direction to avoid the fabric pulling to one side. Measure from the hem upwards at 30 cm (12 in) intervals across the blind to mark the finished length. Trim the excess fabric to 2 cm (¾ in) from the finished length, fold over and pin a strip of touch and close tape to cover the raw edge. Stitch along the top and bottom of the strip.

8. With the blind face down on the table again, insert one rod into each pocket and the lath into the bottom pocket. Stitch the ends of the pockets to close. (When the blind is cleaned the rods can easily slide out of the pockets and be replaced later.)

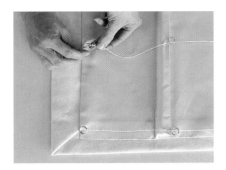

9. Mark the ring positions, starting at 5 cm (2 in) in from each side and allowing three to four rows per width. Stitch the rings securely in position to the top of the rod pockets.

10. Thread the cords from the bottom to the top of the blind, making sure they are long enough to return to the cord holder. Stitch the ends of the cords together to prevent the knots coming undone.

Small recessed windows are difficult to dress in a traditional way with curtains, as curtaining fitted outside rather overpowers the size of the window, while inside it takes most of the light. Roman blinds are the perfect solution, and can be used to dress the window in a subtle way, without interfering with either the shape or the incoming light.

BINDING EDGES

My standard edging size is 1.5 cm (⅝ in). I often adjust it a little either way, slightly less for a fine fabric or a narrow blind and slightly more for a heavy fabric and a wider blind. Order your binding fabrics to be at least the length of the blind so that there are as few joins as possible.

EDGING A LINED OR UNLINED BLIND

1. Cut and join enough strips of 6 cm (2¼ in) wide fabric to bind all the way around. Join strips on the cross to reduce the bulk when the fabric is folded over.

2. Place the blind fabric flat on the worktable, with the right side facing up. Pin the edging strip along one long side as shown. Stop pinning 1.5 cm (⅝ in) from the corner. Fold the edging over at a right angle and continue pinning along the hemline. Repeat with the other corner and side.

3. Stitch all around, at 1.4 cm (just under ⅝ in) from the raw edges. Stop stitching 1.4 cm (just under ⅝ in) from the hem at the corner point. Secure the stitches, fold the fabric flap over and start stitching again at the other side of the point.

4. From the right side, press the edging strip away from the curtain. Fold back under by 1.5 cm (⅝ in), keeping the binding tight against the seam. Mitre the corner and pin in place.

5. Place the blind flat on to the worktable with the right side facing down. Take the pre-prepared linings and at each rod pocket carefully snip the linings so that the lining between the pockets can be unfolded.

6. Place the lining over the main fabric, pockets outwards. Carefully line up the seams and hemline. Pin the sides to hold. Secure each of the pocket stitching lines with pins at right angles to the stitching and with the pockets facing upwards. Stitch along the pocket lines, working from only one direction to avoid pulling to one side. Trim away the excess lining at the sides.

7. Pin the binding edge over the lining and slip stitch all around for a neat finish. Continue to make up the blinds following the instructions from step 6 of the Roman blinds on page 34.

DOUBLE BORDERS

Double borders give a very smart finish, especially when using fabrics in complementary colours. A second binding is added to the first binding before making up or, alternatively, a row of piping is stitched to the blind before adding the flat border.

The deepest shades of blue in the pattern have been picked out with a double border in blue and green.

1. Press a 4 cm (1½ in) strip of the contrast colour in half lengthwise. Stitch to the binding. Stitch both to the blind just inside the first line.

BINDING AN INTERLINED BLIND

1. Place the interlining flat on the worktable and smooth out any creases. Place the blind fabric over the top, right side up. Trim the interlining to the exact size of the fabric. Tack all around and pin these two fabrics together. Make up as steps 1–4 on page 36, treating both fabrics as one.

2. Herringbone the binding around the blind with stitches measuring about 2 cm (¾ in).

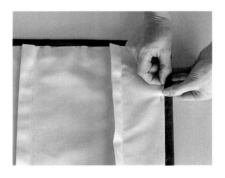

3. Place the lining over the blind, positioning the rod pockets exactly parallel to the hemline, with the lining over the binding, leaving 1.5 cm (⅝ in) showing.

A Roman blind covering a large area can sometimes be boring, so adding pleats to each section gives interesting relief. This style of blind is also very effective with sheer fabrics such as voiles and linens used for light shade or privacy. A plain weave cotton becomes suddenly interesting.

You must first work out the size folds you need for the blind to pull up into the available space. Add 8 cm (3¼ in) to each pleat and make up as normal following the instructions on pages 34–35. Stitch this extra fabric allowance into permanent narrow pleats once the rod pockets have been stitched in place. Vary this idea by designing and making graduating pleats which can create a wonderful cascading effect.

Stripes need to fit the finished blind width exactly. Pleats stitched across the width of a traditional Roman blind create an appealing variation on a standard blind, giving definition and interest, especially when the blind is pulled down.

DESIGN AND MAKE BLINDS

WIDE WINDOWS

Kitchen windows are ideal candidates for Roman blind treatments, often situated above a sink. Blinds cover the window without adding clutter and can so easily be pulled away from sills, taps and utensils. Kitchen windows are often designed to catch as much light as possible and may be too wide for a single blind, so double or even triple blinds should be made. Measure so that each fits within the structure and framework dictated by the window design. The blinds need to be measured and made very accurately to prevent either ugly gaps or fabrics rubbing together.

FAN-SHAPED BLIND

As with many design ideas, this intriguing hem shape is not nearly as complicated to make as it appears. Make up as a straightforward Roman blind, with
a double layer of fabric stitched to make channels for the rods. The lower rods
are split in the centre to form the distinctive fan-shaped hem.

You will just need to estimate how long the blind needs to be made to allow the split rods to form a semi-circular shape.

The radius is half the curtain width, so the distance between the lowest full rod and the sill will need to be equal to half of the window width.

Measure the window and plain rods as for the Roman blind. Cut two layers of linen, silk or cotton the same for the front and back. Slip stitch together along sides and hems. Measure carefully to mark out channels through which the rods can be threaded. Pin every 3–4 cm (1¼–1½ in) to hold both layers of fabric together.

Push the full and half rods into the pockets, slip stitch to close. Stitch brass rings to the back of each pocket and thread cords from bottom to top.

Roman blinds are the ideal solution for some doorways or French windows, where there is little room to draw curtains to either side (right). The rods here have been cut short by approximately 15 cm (6 in) on either side so that the fabric drops to relieve the strict lines. These large blinds are quite dominant when lowered so choose fabric colours which either blend with the walls or have been chosen to form an important part of the overall design.

SHAPED HEMS

The penanted lower edge of the simple checked blind reflects the historical feel and character of this long gallery bedroom and works well with the Medieval print used for the main curtains. The two different coloured checks of the curtain border and the blinds are clever combinations of varying scale and colour.

Roman blinds are chosen to be primarily functional but, as with all home furnishings, they should also be decorative. Making any soft furnishing without proper consideration to design will give a second rate result, as will design without careful making. Adding some shaping to the lower edge is one way of giving some design detail without-out the addition of other colours/fabrics/designs. Simple to design and adaptable to any width or depth, shaped hems need to be drawn and cut sympathetically, to both the architectural style of the window, and the general design of the fabric chosen. I find that some shallow shaping and simple design are possible with most windows, whether tall, short, wide or narrow, even when the blinds drop on to the sill, and especially when a blind is the sole window dressing.

More elaborate designs and shapes can be cut for the hems of blinds which will hang in front of a sill. Deep Gothic shapes could be cut to complement a window in this style. When hems can be more prominent, detail can be more fully emphasised; shapes can be exaggerated and contrasts in colour and texture can be employed imaginatively.

DESIGN AND MAKE BLINDS

Hems can be cut and made using variations of simple geometric forms, for example, circles, triangles and squares. Whatever shape you decide you would like to use for the bottom of your blind, check first that it fits with the overall style and structure of the window frame and pane configuration. Make a paper template from a rough sketch and pin to the window to see the sort of effect your design will have. Adjust the amount of shaping and scale until it seems satisfactory.

MAKING UP

1. Cut a piece of paper, card or a strip of heading buckram the width of the finished blind. Mark the centre and plan each section to be equal, making sure that one section forms the central point of the blind. Measure the strip into the required number of sections, mark the depth of the shaping at the widest and narrowest points. Use a ruler to make even shapes.

2. Cut around the shapes accurately. Pin the template to the window again to check the design and make any alterations.

3. Pin this template to the hemline of the blind fabric and cut around it, allowing 1.5 cm (⅝ in) for the seams. Cut a strip of fabric for the facing, the width of the curtain × the depth of the shaping and up to the first rod. Pin the facing to the blind, with fabrics right sides together. Stitch around the shaped edge, keeping the stitching line 1.4 cm (just under ⅝ in) from the raw edge. Trim seams to just under 1 cm (⅜ in), and snip right into the points.

4. Turn out and press into neat, even shapes. Cut a piece of buckram or other stiffening, exactly the same size as the template. Insert this against the front of the blind. Pin well to secure it in place.

5. Make up your blind following the instructions on page 34-35. If you are using interlining, pin this carefully to the blind fabric and make up as one. The bottom batten pocket will replace the bottom rod position.

6. Stitch the batten pocket, catching in the stiffening with the lower row of stitches.

DOUBLE HEMS

It is quite fun to mix fabrics and styles with double hems. The top fabric is shaped at the hemline with a border made up and stitched behind. A plain colour will show the shaping in relief. We have made up a simple design, showing the front and back of the blind.

HEM IDEAS

These suggestions for hemlines show how effective attention to detail can be. You will need to choose the hem type most suited to your own decoration and room style, but use these ideas as a jumping board to experiment with materials and shapes for your own individual finish.

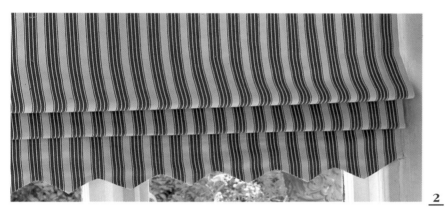

1. Deep shaping is only suitable when the blind will never be fully lowered, or if the blind will fall below a sill. Stunning effects can be created with rope or cord edging, fringing, contrast colours, tassels hanging from each scallop or between each shape.

2. I think this is the simplest edge shape to make. Points can be made deeper, shallower, narrower, wider, to suit any window treatment. The lower edge could be finished with piping stitched between the blind and the facing, or with cord hand stitched in place once the blind is complete.

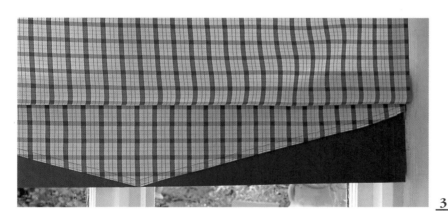

3. A smart treatment, the blind edge could have been more heavily top stitched or made with an inset border following the diagonal lines. The dark green under skirt emphasises the shaping.

4. The combination of scallops and points should be hand drawn on to paper to make a rough template. Experiment with any combination of angular or curved geometric shapes. Mixing checks, stripes and prints in similar tones of greens and off-whites make a strong statement.

SCALLOPED HEMS

Hemlines shaped to gently rounded or deeply curved scallops provide interesting detail, especially for fabrics printed in soft patterns as there are no sharp corners or angles to go against the flow. Pipe the edges in a small complementary check, stripe or toning plain fabric for a truly professional finish.

MAKING SCALLOPS

1. Scallops should be even in size and the best way to cut an accurate hemline is to make a template. Cut a piece of card or a strip of heading buckram the width of the blind. Mark into sections for each scallop. In addition, mark the size of the scallop at the widest and narrowest points. Draw around a household object to define the first shape. Either trace this first one and use it to copy from or continue to use the same saucer, plate or bowl. Cut out the shaped edge accurately.

2. Pin this template to the main fabric and draw around it carefully.

3. Cut the main fabric around the shaping, allowing 1.5 cm (⅝ in) for seams. Cut a strip of fabric for the facing, the width of the blind and the depth from the bottom of the scallop to the first rod/bottom batten. Pin this facing to the blind with right sides together. Pin around the scallops, then stitch slowly around each one, keeping the stitching line 1.4 cm (just under ⅝ in) from the raw edge. Trim the seam to 1 cm (⅜ in) and snip right into the points. Snip the curves at approximately 1 cm (⅜ in) intervals.

4. Turn out and press into even, rounded shapes. Cut a piece of facing or stiffening to the exact size of the template and insert it, to lie against the blind. Pin together. Make up the blind following the instructions on pages 34-35. The flat batten will take the place of the bottom rod. Stitch the facing over the lining to make a pocket so that the batten fits snugly. Insert the batten and slip stitch the side openings neatly together.

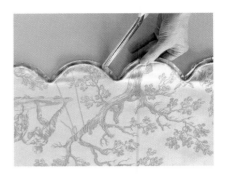

5. If you wish to pipe the scallops, make up enough piping for the whole job and pin around the scalloped edging on the blind fabric, 1.4 cm (just under ⅝ in) from the raw edge, snipping where necessary so that the piping lies flat. Bend the piping sharply into the points and pin. Stitch around as closely to the piping as possible for a neat finish.

6. Cut a facing in the same fabric to fit from the bottom of the scallop to the top of the batten pocket. Pin to the main fabric with right sides together and stitch tight to the piping line. Trim the seam to 1 cm (⅜ in), snip as necessary, turn out and press.

Soft scallops create an elegant hemline to this classic blind and offset the simple and uncluttered lines of this window treatment.

HEMS AND EDGINGS

The checked hem of this pretty half blind adds definition without detracting from the hand-printed olive leaf pattern.

Blinds don't need added hems and borders to be functional, and in previous pages I have shown many blinds looking perfect without. But the art of creating a home has much to do with attention to detail, so hems and edgings openly and extensively provide this opportunity.

Designing interesting and individual finishes to add to your blinds and curtains is not just an indulgent excuse to choose more lovely fabrics and trimmings or to try out another idea, but an important bridge from average to special.

Always remember that a detail should be just that. Whatever finish you choose must in some way enhance the window treatment and the overall room design, and not in any way push itself to the forefront to take over or detract from any other item. This checked border is vital to this window treatment with layers of lightweight fabrics, in defining the extent of the blind. Clever in the way that it breaks the almost freefall effect of the printed design, picking up the tones while matching nothing, and remaining so subtle as to be almost incidental to the finished result.

Adding hems and edgings can prolong the life of blinds and also curtains, especially useful if you need to move house regularly. Borders and hems are a good disguise when adapting a blind to a larger window. Similarly, a new hem or border can change the style.

On pages 60–63 there are ideas for stencilling and appliqué, which are eminently adaptable to decorate borders and hems. The secret is to make any addition look as though it were originally planned.

The checked border on the blind overleaf was chosen to complement the main fabric, picking up the tones of the hand printed olive leaves and adding visual weight to the design. Jute scrim and white linen go along with the natural, open feel. The same check has also been picked up for the armchair, sofa and cushions in the room. Blinds need not be made to function fully, especially if the curtains are substantial enough, and this one has been made up as a 'half blind', performing the valuable function of blocking an unwanted and unattractive aspect.

Buttons and borders provide alternative hem details, offering the chance to introduce a change of scale or a splash of colour. Experiment with checks and stripes, patterns and checks, plains in contrasting or toning colours, plains with patterns, until you find a combination which is pleasing to the eye in scale and tonal value. Buttons, eyelets, ribbons, strings, even buckles, make interesting applied details to decorate blinds.

BUTTONED AND APPLIED HEM

These blinds will be made up in exactly the same way as described on page 34–35, with one adaption – the bottom batten will be fitted in the position of the bottom rod instead of the base of the blind. When you calculate the rod positions, remember to make

allowance for the decorative hem detail to hang well below the folds when the blind is raised. An attached hem should add weight and be heavy enough in its own right not to curl and buckle. You might need to slip a length of chain weight along the bottom of the hem if the fabric does not hang as well as you would like.

MAKING UP

1. Make up blind following instructions on pages 34–35, leaving the fabrics free at the hemline.

2. Cut a strip of another fabric the width of the blind, plus 2 cm (¾ in) at each side for the seams × 4 times the finished depth. Press this piece of fabric in half length-wise, right sides inside. Open out and press each side to the centre. Open out and pin three sides together and make 1.8 cm (just under ¾ in) seams on both short sides.

3. Trim across the corner and trim the seam to 1 cm (⅜ in).

4. Turn out and press. Fold the fabric to the inside along the previously pressed lines.

5. Check the depth of the lowest section of the blind and trim the hemline so that all layers are level. Stitch along the lower edge to hold the fabrics together.

6. Sleeve the folded fabric over and pin in position. Attach to the main fabric with buttons or other type of applied decoration, making sure that the stitching goes right through to hold the applied hem firmly in place.

1. A denim border contrasts with unbleached artists' linen used for the main blind and fastened with men's coat buttons. Any decorative buttoning could be used and the fabrics could be plain with a pattern, a check with a stripe.

2. Attach tabs of fabric or tape and a contrast fabric to the blind hem. Stitch the raw edges together to secure and sandwich into the folded denim. Fabric-covered buttons add the finishing touch.

3. I suppose this hem is attached rather than applied but is still relevant to the purpose of considering what other hem options might be possible. The blind hem needed to be finished and a narrow batten inserted for weight. Follow the instructions given to make the shaped edge for the 'applied hem'. Slip stitch the top edge together. Make holes and fit eyelets as shown in the kit instructions and thread through cord, knotting the ends.

4. Another way to use a scalloped edge. Cut the shapes and make up the blind hem with piping as shown on page 46. Make up the applied hem as shown, but instead of sleeving it over, slide it under the scalloped edge and hand-stitch the scallops to the hem, making small and neat stitches between the main fabric and the piping.

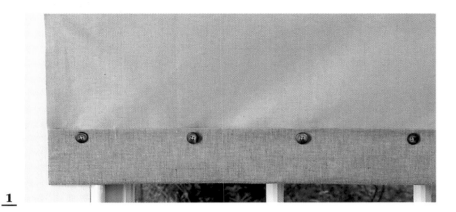

BOUGHT EDGINGS

The simplest Roman blind can be lifted with the addition of a bought trimming. Fringes, fan edgings, braids, tassels and gimps are available from interior decorators and furnishing fabric specialists in any combination of colours, styles and price which you could possibly want.

Choose edgings to subtly blend with the main fabric colours or to provide a complete contrast – whichever is most in keeping with the general furnishing style and fabric design. Should you really not be able to find the perfect finish, ask your interior decorator to design and organise trimmings to be made especially. This is only viable for large projects, but well worth the extra trouble if the blind is part of a larger furnishing project with curtains and pelmets.

I was very fortunate to find several pieces of hand-worked lace in an antique clothes shop. These had all probably experienced their first life attached to the sleeves and hems of night wear but I have made some feminine finishes for blinds, curtains and bed cushions.

I always like to stitch antique lace leaving the unevenness of the hand made tops showing. Simple embroidered knots hold the lace in place and suit the character of the toile de jouy – this particular one is a traditional design called 'le serment d'aimer' which roughly translates as 'the promise of love'.

These blinds have been made up in a modern toile de jouy, with flowers and cherubs entwined in classical scrolls to show four edgings in toning threads of linen, cotton and silk, emphasising the effect of using different passementerie styles and shapes.

1. Cut silk fringe is always an elegant trimming and, if it has a pretty top, should be stitched to the front of the blind.

2. Linen fan edging inserted between the main fabric and lining adds interest to the hemline, allowing the fabric to predominate.

3. Stitch cord over a finished blind in any shape and design you might choose. This idea can work wonders in rejuvenating an old blind and can be further employed should a blind need lengthening at any stage later in its life.

4. The best passementerie is hand made. This one was made in France and incorporates wooden 'olives' – turned wooden oval balls are traditional decoration, painted or stained and sometimes covered with silk threads. The pretty top deserves to be admired.

1

2

3

4

DESIGN IDEAS

These curtains are fitted to the same pole as the blind and are for decorative use only. A batten for the blind fittings is hidden just behind the pole and the cords extend behind the curtain to operate the blinds.

Mixing and matching fabrics, experimenting with unusual and individual colour combinations, textures and techniques, can be sheer joy and relaxation for the confirmed fabri-holic. To develop an 'eye' for what is good design and to understand your own taste, takes time and experience. So begin a scrap book, and fill it with torn-out pages from magazines, colours and fabric combinations, carpet and paint charts, anything which you find pleasing. Then, when you are ready to start designing and making your furnishings, you will have references to help you.

Using blinds with curtains is always a winning combination for a special window treatment. I always like to fit blinds behind curtains to give an extra dimension. Decoratively, long curtains add elegance and proportion to a room which is always missing when curtains are short, but practically, the current fashion for situating radiators immediately below window sills causes a problem. Here, blinds really come into their own. Made along with curtains, often in the same fabric, and covering the window at night, blinds allow the maximum heat to radiate, while long curtains can be draped back to fulfil the decorative criteria.

Some ideas to whet your appetite, inspire and encourage you are shown over the next few pages. Stencilling, patchwork, appliqué and quilting are simple techniques that everyone can master, with or without the borders and edgings shown previously. Remember that the key to successful designing and making is the attention to detail, from the scale of a printed pattern to the exact tone of the piping. Consider, also, that any design you dream up will need to look as good when the blind is raised as when it is lowered.

Checks cut on the cross, combined with those on the straight, demonstrate the range of exciting design ideas you can try on your own windows. A gentle frill softens the sharp lines and strong image of the checks.

Soft furnishings and fashion are much more aligned than is generally realised. A blue gingham shirt caught my eye on a shopping trip this summer, and became my inspiration when I designed this blind.

To make this blind, divide the finished width into three sections, adding 1.5 cm (⅝ in) seam and 6 cm (2¼ in) side allowances to each. Cut the outer sections with the straight of the grain and the centre section on the cross. Cut lining pieces to match, but keep to the grain with each. Stitch the centre lining and fabric sections together. Stitch piping along the seam allowance. Stitch the two outer fabric sections and lining together along the side which will join to the centre section. Fold over the fabric side allowances and herringbone to keep in place. Trim the lining back and fold under to leave 4 cm (1½ in) of main fabric showing. Stitch the three pieces together. Cut two strips of lining the length of the blind × 5 cm (2 in). Fold into four lengthwise and bind the two seams. Make up the frill for the lower edge and add to the blind, binding the raw edges.

Stitch the heading and then the rings in place and thread the cords through. Cut a rod the width of the finished blind, cover with fabric and stitch to the outer edge and seams just above the frill.

Sometimes constructing your own fabric is much more dramatic and fun than buying a printed design. Lengths of white and yellow cotton chintz were cut into accurate squares and then stitched together in a diagonal pattern to make this dynamic flat blind.

An all-round bordered edge confines the design and the hem border gives an interesting change of scale. However the design is worked out, keep the centre line and symmetry correct. Use the same fabric idea for cushions, throws or tablecloths.

Combine colours to create your own fabric. Bright yellow and white cotton squares have been stitched into a regular diamond pattern to form the basis for this vivid, modern blind.

Left: An artistic window treatment features a scalloped blind with an organza curtain tied in a plump knot.

Above: Fabric used for a Roman blind has also been put into service as the lining for these simple curtains.

Right: An elegant window dressing mixes fabrics and styles and the soft, unrodded blind has been designed to disappear completely under the pelmet if required. Once again, fabric for both the blind and curtain lining are the same for a unified effect.

Sometimes a blind is the ideal solution for the window treatment, but the window itself is not a good feature, and needs to be dressed or softened.

In this room (above), we needed to design a blind which could easily be raised and lowered as required for privacy, but we found that there were times when the blind needed to be raised to allow light into the room yet some privacy was still required. An organza curtain hung directly in front of the blind provided the solution, and tying it

in the centre gave an interesting dimension to the blind. The 'pelmet' was simply a straight piece of fabric bound, lined and tied to brass hooks pinned to a fabric covered back-board.

Curtains and blinds can prove a winning combination, especially when you provide something which links the two. The intimate and relaxing corner (above right) has been achieved by lining a pair of simple curtains with the same fabric as that used to make the Roman blind and cushion for the window seat.

A soft Roman blind, that is made up as instructions on pages 34–35 but without battens, can be raised to completely disappear behind the pelmet drape (right). A simple, but very elegant treatment created using the most basic fabric, as crisp white cotton is lined in navy and white ticking and edged in denim looks incredibly smart. Making a blind and lining the curtains in the same fabric adds a professional finish, and always looks good, especially when the curtains are tied back to reveal the lining whenever the blind is down.

DECORATIVE FINISHES

Because of their nature, blinds are perfect for further embellishment with other decorative techniques. This blind made from inexpensive fabric has been stencilled to create a very individual design. You can buy a pre-cut stencil or make your own.

The simplest fabrics and blinds can be transformed into the most individual and creative window treatments, and even works of art in their own right, using techniques such as stencilling, hand embroidery, appliqué and quilting, to name but a few. Over the next few pages, you can see how calico has been upgraded completely using basic shapes, appliqué and stencils – fun treatments which will give you inspiration for small windows, short term window treatments and difficult areas such as cloakrooms, nurseries, utility rooms, tack rooms, flower rooms and corridors. Quilting brings life to the most modest and eternal of fabrics: ginghams and tickings, and these can be combined happily with appliquéd and stencilled designs. The extra padding will keep any window draught-free. In fact, this stencilled blind (right) was the least expensive blind to make in the whole book and I think one of the most usable ideas, adaptable to all windows and rooms.

Piping the edge just gives an almost invisible and elegant finish. If you have other skills which you can add to blinds to show off your prowess, spend some time playing with ideas and designs so you will be able to make completely individual soft furnishings.

The appliquéd finish (above) is as suitable for a toddler as a teenager. Stencilling (right) offers a different effect. Whether intricate or simple, shells, boats or waves are fun for bathrooms.

Blinds not only offer an excellent opportunity for finishes and details, but also the choice to employ other craft techniques such as quilting, embroidery, appliqué and stencilling. Any one of these can give your blind a truly individual and creative flourish.

Whichever finish you choose to use, all embellishment must be completed on the fabric before the blind is made up. First, mark the finished dimensions of the blind on to the main fabric with coloured tacks to define the top and bottom, left and right – these must be accurate lines which you need to work within.

Some processes, especially quilting, require an extra percentage of fabric to allow for 'shrinkage'. An average allowance is 10 per cent but if you want to quilt deeply add 20 per cent to the estimated amount of fabric.

STENCILLING

Perhaps stencil a basket of fruit for a kitchen blind, or some drying herbs, a teddy bear or a futuristic motor for a child's bedroom, vines and grapes for a dining room.

So many stencils are available to purchase, whether mass produced machine cut or hand cut individual designs, from a simple bow to the most elaborate bough of magnolia flowers, classical scrolls and Greek key patterns or Christmas trees and bows and bells for celebrations.

Always stencil on to fabrics which have been pre-washed, and make sure you only use paint which has been specifically formulated for fabrics. Fabric paint is readily available from good haberdashery outlets, craft or needlework shops.

QUILTING

Fabrics take on a different dimension when quilted: checks and stripes come to life, patterns can be traced around with machine or hand stitches, simple glazed or brushed cotton quilted in squares can look as luxurious as brushed suede.

Hand quilters might like to follow one of the traditional bed quilt designs as a striking window blind. Sandwich 50 g or 100 g (2 oz or 4 oz) terylene wadding between your top fabric and a lining of tightly woven cotton. Tack all around, across the centres and at approximately 15 cm (6 in) intervals before stitching your chosen design.

Quilting blinds (right) makes them very warm and cosy and ideal to use under unlined curtains. Pulled up in the summer, this blind acts as a wonderful draught excluder in the cold and windy winter months.

Chintz in three tones of yellow with tweed make an effective 'sunflower' appliqué. The bound edge defines the area and is matched to one of the appliqué colours.

APPLIQUÉ

Simple shapes show how effective appliqué can be on folded blinds. Children's bedrooms and playrooms respond well to simple shapes which can be stitched by even a complete beginner. Use children's books to copy simplistic shapes, half-moons, stars, teddy bears, cats and other animals.

Choose fabric which has a light weave and frays as little as possible. Draw your design on to tracing paper, cut out the shapes and pin to the fabric. Cut around the tracing paper shapes.

Pin very close together across the raw edge, so that the pins can remain in place during stitching. Machine stitch edgings to cover the raw edges. Usually a colour which tones with the cut pieces is easier to handle as any slight errors in direction will then not be too noticeable.

LONDON BLINDS

I chose to use a simple mattress ticking in a formal colour combination, and buttoned the folds with dark green chintz-covered tailors' buttons. The structured style reminds me of a smart jacket back and the presentation of this blind is as good raised as it is lowered.

London blinds are made in the same manner as Austrian or cascade blinds, with the fullness being incorporated into pleats. These pleats look stunning if they are made using a contrasting plain fabric as they just pop open slightly when the gathers are formed, as though revealing a secret. Plan the cutting, the pleats and the swags carefully before you start to order fabrics. Follow the instructions and directions on page 28. The hemlines can be treated really extravagantly with fringes and tassels, and this treatment will bring out the best of quite outrageous fabrics, however strong the colouring and design. London blinds can be made with little fullness to be quite minimal or with masses of fullness incorporated into the pleats which will burst out as the blind is raised. The higher the blind, the fuller the fabric and the more blousy the effect.

AUSTRIAN BLINDS

The desk below the window enables the garden to be enjoyed while working and provides a convenient place for seasonal gift wrapping.

Austrian blinds were originally called festoons, and were designed during the 18th century for decoration only to embellish very practical, shuttered windows. Later, they became functional as pull-up single curtains and covered the window completely, finishing at either skirting or dado level. Little fullness was used, as fabrics were wool, heavy cotton or damask and weighted with the addition of elaborately fringed hems.

In the last ten years, the concept of pull-up curtains has been rejuvenated with the ornate use of fabrics and trimmings available from today's extensive source of materials.

Austrian blinds can be made very full if lightweight silks or cottons are used, but sides and hems should not be over-filled. Instead, finish with one of the many detailed trimmings or hand stitching.

This interesting and unusual window treatment, comprising two different blinds using similar fabrics, was designed for a country office. I first decided on a Roman blind which would be easy to operate, taking up little space and with the tremendous plus point that these blinds can be positioned at any level to cut glare from the sun while working. But Roman blinds can be quite severe and I felt a more feminine finish was needed. An Austrian blind over the top proves a good alternative to the more obvious pelmet solution.

Austrian blinds are more correctly pull-up curtains. The fullness, as with a curtain, is across the width, but the fabric is cut to be overlong, leaving the bottom 30 cm (12 in) or so in folds which drape in swags according to the amount of fullness allowed.

Traditionally, fabrics such as wool bombazine, silk damask and woven cotton were used, with very little fullness allowed and little ornamentation. A fringed braid would be stitched to the lower edge so that the swagged hemline hung well. Later, blinds became fuller and more heavily decorated with fringes, cords and tassels. Headings were also swagged or covered with draped pelmets.

Austrian blinds can be made with very little fullness (above). Pleated headings at each scallop add just enough fullness for soft drapes while allowing the pattern to remain as a picture. We added goblet pleats at each end and at each scallop. The scarlet blind (right) demonstrates how gathers bring out the best qualities of a plain fabric as the light and shadow play on the folds, enriching the colour and weave.

Austrian blinds can be made with little or much fullness, depending how you want them to look. Use lightweight silks or cottons for a really opulent effect, heavier-weight cottons or wools for a more formal look. Follow the instructions on page 10 to plan and estimate the shape you are looking for and on page 15 to estimate the amount of fabric and edgings to order.

MAKING UP

1. Place the blind fabric right side facing down on to the worktable. Turn over the sides and hem by 10 cm (4 in) and pin to hold. Mitre the corner as explained on page 8, and herringbone the sides and hem in place.

2. Place the lining on the blind fabrics, matching the seams. Lock stitch the seams together.

3. Fold the lining over along the stitched raw edge and trim 4 cm (1½ in) in from trim line. Turn under 2 cm (¾ in) and pin, leaving 8 cm (3¼ in) of the main fabric showing all round.

4. Slip stitch all round and press lightly. Measuring from the bottom upwards, and at 30 cm (12 in) intervals across the blind, mark the overall drop. Fold the fabric and lining over along the overall drop line and pin.

5. Mark the ring positions following your original plan. Always measure each one from the bottom of the blind upwards to avoid any errors. The outer row will be on the lining edge and the others at equal intervals between. It is always best to make one row along each seam line. Allow an average spacing of 10–20 cm (4–8 in) between each ring.

6. Gather up the blind in your hands and test how close together the gathers should be for your window. Stitch each ring into the lining two or three times, pick up threads from the front, stitch again into the lining, wind the thread round and double stitch to fasten off securely.

7. Thread the cords through from the bottom ring upwards, knotting and stitching the cords together at the lowest ring. Trim the heading as necessary.

MAKING UP HEADINGS

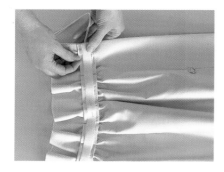

1. For a gathered heading, fold over 5–7 cm (2–3 in) and pin gathering tape to cover the raw edge. Stitch, then pull up to the finished width. Cut a strip of lining the length of the finished width plus 4 cm (1½ in) for turnings and three times the depth of the tape. Stitch fastening tape to the centre. Press the two sides under to make a band just wider than the tape. Slip stitch the band securely covering the heading tape.

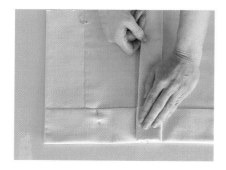

2. For a pleated heading, trim the fabric and lining to double the depth of the required pleats above the overall drop line. Fold under double and pin. Slip stitch the open sides down. Mark the gap and pleat widths along the top of the blind. Stitch each pleat, press and stitch down.

Fan-edged braid adds shape and colour to a frilled edge, and a gathered heading is made more interesting with knotted cords in the same tones. Some braids have a decorative top so these might be better stitched to the front of the blind. A fan-edged braid with a plain top should be stitched on before the frill and sandwiched between the fabric and the lining.

HEMS AND HEADINGS

Much of the character of an Austrian blind is determined by the fullness and the manner in which this fullness is contained at the heading and decorated at the hem. The heading can be pleated, gathered or trimmed with ribbon or braid, while the hemline might be kept plain, bordered with a contrast fabric, frilled or decorated with bought trimmings.

1. Austrian blinds will hang more evenly if the hemline is weighted in some way. The degree of weight needed should be considered with the size of the blind. A heavy fabric will warrant a deep bullion fringe, whereas a light fabric can be weighted effectively with a light linen or silk fringe. Trimmings made with similar combinations of colours to those of the main fabric, such as these here, add detail which is subtle and often more compatible with the overall room scheme than a simple contrasting colour. The formal lines dictated by the strong stripes are contained within a discreet pleated heading.
2. Austrian blinds are in themselves full enough for the fabric to be greatly enriched with the light and shadow play of the horizontal and vertical gathers. Adding more frills will more often than not detract from the whole point of making an Austrian blind. Sometimes you see blinds with the sides and hem all frilled. These blinds can be rather

1

DESIGN AND MAKE BLINDS

overpowering, so take care of the size and fullness of the frilled edging. A deeply frilled hem is perhaps best, giving enough additional weight to the blind and added interest. Just one-and-a-half times fullness prevents the frill becoming too dominant and the ribbon edging strengthens the style. The simple gathered heading has also been finished with a row of ribbed ribbon.

3. Blanket stitch is probably the one stitch which every child learns to sew during the first few school years. It is very simple and easy to learn, but very effective. Use a thickness of thread suited to the main fabric; here, we used a medium weight wool for the heavy cotton and a stitch size proportionate with the blind size and the strength of the fabric. Threading the heading on to a

pole is an effective treatment, no matter how much fullness has been included. Stitch a casing which measures half the circumference of the pole plus a little extra for ease, about 5 cm (2 in) from the top of the blind. Thread the pole through the casing, gathering the fabric evenly. The fixing batten needs to be fitted to the wall immediately below the pole.

FESTOON BLINDS

Festoon blinds are chosen mainly for the decorative effect achieved by the tight gathers and swagged hemline. The fabric can be cut between 50 per cent and 200 per cent wider than the window and up to 300 per cent longer.

Festoon blinds are by their nature, very feminine window treatments – full of flounce and frill. The fabric can be cut up to 200 per cent wider and 300 per cent longer than the window for a really opulent effect. The fullest width and fullest length will result in a very richly gathered, opulent blind. Instead of a frilled hemline you could add a deep cut fringe or bullion.

Traditional fabrics are wool and silk in plain weaves or woven with a damask design. Used extensively in the 18th century, the blinds would often be made up from the same fabric used to upholster the walls and finished with richly ornate handmade passementerie. The festoon blind shown here is rich and opulent, with a deep frill and bounteous swags. It is a popular style of festoon, and a sharp contrast to the blind shown overleaf, which comprises organza layers in vivid shades of red.

Experiment with feminine fabrics and colours when making a festoon blind. Layers of silk organza in scarlet, powder pink and apricot (left) may seem an unlikely combination, but give interesting effects with the light play on the gathers.

MAKING UP

1. Place the fabric on to the work-table, right side facing down. Turn in the sides 7 cm (3 in) and press.

2. Cut strips of fabric 15 cm (6 in) wide and twice the width of the blind, and join together. Fold in half lengthwise and run a gathering thread 1.5 cm (⅝ in) from the raw edge.

3. Divide the blind into ten sections and mark each with a marking tack. Repeat with the frill.

4. Unpick the thread 3 cm (1¼ in) from each end of the frill and stitch half of the frill to the blind, with the folded edge against the 6 cm (2¼ in) side fold as shown. Snip the blind 1.5 cm (⅝ in) to meet the edge of the frill.

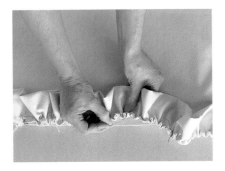

5. Pull up the gathering threads. Pin the corresponding marking tacks together and distribute gathers evenly between.

6. Fold the sides over again and herringbone all around the sides and the hem to hold them in place. Slip stitch the edge of the frill to enclose the raw edges.

7. Place the blind back on to the worktable, right side down and place the lining over, matching the seams. Score the lining along the folded edge and trim the lining away 4 cm (1½ in) from this line.

8. Slip stitch the lining along the frill to enclose all raw edges.

9. Pin narrow blind tape to cover the lining raw edge, on each seam, and as many times across each width as planned. Pull out the cord so it remains free of the heading tape and tuck the ends of the tapes underneath.

10. Pull up the heading tape and the vertical tapes. Thread cords through from bottom to top, knotting and stitching the ends.

CARE FOR BLINDS

Washing / cleaning

Unlined blinds are usually used in areas which will need regular cleaning and should be washed or dry cleaned in accordance with manufacturer's instructions. If frequent washing is essential, use a strong, hardwearing fabric like cotton, with enough substance to stand regular handling. Soft blinds such as Austrian, cascade or rolled up blinds should be used; rolled up blinds being the most suitable as there will be no rods or rings to remove before cleaning. To prevent a shrinkage problem, either wash the fabric before making up or over-cut the drops and make up with the shrinkage allowance so that this will be taken up at the first wash. Make sure that every trace of detergent is removed as sunlight will react with the chemicals to cause fading. Always press while still damp as pressing and steaming will keep the fabric in shape. Try not to press over seams, only press up to them with the point of the iron. If you do need to press over a seam, slip a piece of cloth beween the seam and the main fabric to prevent a ridge forming.

Airing

The best and most effective way to keep window treatments clean and fresh is to choose a slightly breezy day, open the windows wide, close the blinds and allow them to blow in the breeze for a few hours. This will remove the slightly musty lining smell. If you can do this every few weeks your blinds will always stay 'fresh'. Although this may be more of a problem in the confines of a busy city, it is possible if you choose a quiet, breezy spring or autumn Sunday or holiday.

Vacuuming

The regular removal of dust is vital to prevent particles settling into the fabric grain, as once dirt has penetrated it is very difficult and often impossible to remove with any satisfaction.

Vacuum all soft furnishings regularly with a soft brush, paying special attention to the inside of pleats and frills. For delicate fabrics and pelmets make a muslin or fine calico 'mob cap', elasticated to fit over the end of the brush to soften the bristle-fabric abrasion. Use a gentle suction, available on most types of cleaner.

Dry cleaning

Clean interlined and Roman blinds only if essential or before alterations. Regular care and attention will prevent blinds from becoming 'dirty'. Remove the rods and battens by unpicking the stitches from one side. If you have used brass rings, ask your dry cleaner if these need to be removed also. The cords will probably need to be changed completely as constant use does make them grey, and they are impossible to clean satisfactorily.

Alterations

If blinds need to be altered for any reason like moving house, have them cleaned by a specialist dry cleaner before alterations are carried out.

GLOSSARY

FIBRES

Acrylic Manmade from petrol, often mixed with more expensive fibres to keep the cost down. Not hardwearing, but useful for permanent pleating.

Cotton A natural fibre, cotton is very versatile, woven, knitted and mixed with other fibres. It will lose strength in direct sunlight, so protect. Soft, strong, easy to launder, washable if pre-shrunk.

Linen Fibres found inside the stalks of the flax plant are woven to make linen cloth in almost any weight. Distinctive slub weave from very fine linen for under-curtains and sheers to heavy upholstery weight. A very strong fibre which is easy to work and will take high temperatures.

Silk From the cocoon of the silk worm, silk is soft and luxurious to touch. Fades in sunlight, so protect. Available in every weight, suitable for soft furnishings.

Wool A natural fibre, liable to excessive shrinkage as the 'scales' on each fibre overlap, harden and 'felt'. Is warm to touch and initially resists damp.

Viscose Wood pulp woven into fibres which mixes well with other fibres helping them to take dyes and fireproofing. Washable and sheds dirt easily.

FABRICS

Brocade Traditionally woven fabric using silk, cotton, wool or mixed fibres, on a jacquard loom, in a multi or self coloured floral design. Some are washable but most will need dry cleaning.

Calico Coarse, plain weave cotton in cream or white with 'natural' flecks in it. Available in many widths and weights. Wash before use to shrink and press while damp.

Cambric Closely woven, plain weave fabric from linen or cotton with a sheen on one side. Use, wash and press as Calico.

Canvas Plain weave cotton in various weights. Available as unbleached, coarse cotton or more finely woven and dyed in strong colours.

Chintz Cotton fabric with Eastern design using flowers and birds, often with a resin finish which gives a characteristic sheen or glaze and which also repels dirt. The glaze will eventually wash out, so only dry clean curtains. Avoid using steam to press and never fold or the glaze will crack.

Corduroy A strong fabric woven to form vertical ribs by floating extra yarn across which is then cut to make the pile. Press on a velvet pinboard while damp.

Crewel Plain or hopsack woven, natural cotton background embroidered in chain stitch in plain cream wool or multi-coloured wools. Soft but heavy; may be washed, but test a small piece first.

Damask A jacquard fabric first woven in Damascus with satin floats on a warp satin background in cotton, silk, wool and mixed fibres in various weights. Make up reversed if a matt finish is required.

Gingham Plain weave fabric with equal width stripes of white plus one other colour in both warp and weft threads to produce blocks of checks or stripes in 100% cotton. Mix with floral patterns and other checks and stripes.

Holland Firm, hardwearing fabric made from cotton or linen stiffened with oil or shellac.

Lace Open work fabrics in designs ranging from simple spots to elaborate panels. Usually in cotton or a cotton/polyester mix.

Moiré A finish usually on silk or acetate described as 'water-marked'. The characteristic moiré markings are produced by pressing plain woven fabric through hot engraved cylinders which crush the threads and push them into different directions to form the pattern. This finish will disappear on contact with water.

Muslin White or off-white, inexpensive, open-weave cloth which can be dyed in pastel colours.

Organdie The very finest cotton fabric with an acid finish giving it a unique crispness. Wash and press while damp.

Organza Similar to organdie and made of silk, polyester or viscose. Use layers of varying tones or pastel colours over each other.

Provençal prints Small print designs printed by hand on to fine cotton. Washable, hard wearing, soft and easy to work with.

Silk shantung Light to medium-weight silk woven with irregular yarns giving a dull, rough appearance. Available in an extensive range of colours, gathers and frills.

Taffeta Woven from silk, acetate and blends. Used for elaborate drapes because it handles well and for its light-reflecting qualities.

Tartan Authentic tartans belong to individual Scottish clans and are woven or worsted fine twill weave with an elaborate checked design. Traditional wool tartans are hardwearing.

Ticking Characteristic original herringbone weave in black and white, now woven in many colours and weights. Not usually pre-shrunk.

Toile de jouy Pastoral designs in one colour printed on to calico using copper plate printing techniques.

Tweed Wool or worsted cloth in square or rectangular checked designs in few colours.

Velvet Originally 100% silk, now made from cotton, viscose or other manmade fibres. Woven with a warp pile and additional yarn in loops which are up to 3 mm (⅛ in) depth to form a pile. Care needs to be taken when sewing or the fabrics will 'walk'. Press on a velvet pinboard. Dry clean carefully. Always buy good quality velvet with a dense pile which will not pull out easily.

Voile Fine, light plain weave cotton or polyester fabric dyed in many plain colours. Easily washable and little pressing necessary.

INDEX